This book belongs to

_____

I am VERY special to God!

When Should? I Pray?

Written by Nancy Elizabeth Pharr
Illustrated by Heidi Rose

WestBow Press books may be ordered through booksellers or by contacting:

WestBow Press
A Division of Thomas Nelson & Zondervan
1663 Liberty Drive
Bloomington, IN 47403
www.westbowpress.com
1 (866) 928-1240

Because of the dynamic nature of the Internet, any web addresses or links contained in this book may have changed since publication and may no longer be valid. The views expressed in this work are solely those of the author and do not necessarily reflect the views of the publisher, and the publisher hereby disclaims any responsibility for them.

Any people depicted in stock imagery provided by Thinkstock are models, and such images are being used for illustrative purposes only. Certain stock imagery © Thinkstock.

Interior Image Credit: Heidi Rose

ISBN: 978-1-5127-9793-0 (sc)
ISBN: 978-1-5127-9794-7 (e)

Library of Congress Control Number: 2017911874

Print information available on the last page.

WestBow Press rev. date: 11/14/2018

WESTBOW
PRESS®
A DIVISION OF THOMAS NELSON
& ZONDERVAN

*In gratitude to
my grandmother,
the late Mrs. Addie Marie Haggard,
for teaching me to pray,
and for being such a
positive role model
in my spiritual walk.*

When should I pray?

Pray in the morning
as you greet the sun.

8

Pray at night when the day is done.

9

Pray at mealtime before you eat.

Pray in the car when you take your seat.

11

Pray whenever you lose your way.

Pray anytime of the night or day.

Pray when you meet
someone sick or alone.

14

Pray for all the people
who have no home.

Pray when you have any problem at all.

16

Pray when you're on top,
and pray when you fall.

17

Pray when you don't have
any special reason.

Pray any day of each
and every season.

Pray when you feel happy;
pray when you feel sad.

20

Pray when you are sorry for doing something bad.

Pray that God will help you
to be kind and good.

22

Pray because you want to,
not because you should.

Pray whenever you need a friend.

24

Pray when you want the hurt to end.

Pray at any age, at two or ninety-two.

Pray when you don't know
exactly what to do.

27

Pray in your yard or
pray in your house.

Pray out loud or be quiet as a mouse.

29

Pray in a crowd or alone in your room.

30

Pray when you're cleaning
and pushing a broom.

Pray when you take a short ride on your bike.

32

Pray when you go with your friend on a hike.

33

Pray to give
God thanks
and praise.

34

God tells us in the Bible to pray ALWAYS!

Prayers I Can Say

When I Get Up

Good morning, God!
Thank you for this new day!
Please bless my Mommy
    and Daddy.
Please bless my family.
Please bless me and all the
    people in the world.
I love you, God!
Help me to be good today.
Amen.

Before I Eat

Thank you for the world so sweet.
Thank you for the food we eat.
Thank you for the birds that sing.
Thank you, God, for everything! Amen.
(Traditional)

36

When I Want to Say "I Love You"

Dear God,
you are my Heavenly Father.
You take care of me and everyone
    else in the whole world.
You are very good.
I love you very much! Amen.

Our Father

Our Father, who art in heaven,
    hallowed be thy name.
Thy kingdom come.
Thy will be done on earth
    as it is in heaven.
Give us this day
    our daily bread,
and forgive us our trespasses,
    as we forgive those
    who trespass against us.
And lead us not into temptation;
    but deliver us from evil. Amen.

When I Want to Say "Thank You"

Thank you, God, for you!
Thank you, God, for making me.
Thank you, God, for loving me.
You give me so many good gifts!
Thank you for my Mommy and Daddy.
Thank you for my family and friends.
Thank you for our beautiful world. Amen.

When I'm Sick

Dear God,
I feel sick today.
I don't want to play.
I don't want to eat or talk.
Please make me feel
        better soon. Amen.

When I Want to Say "I'm Sorry"

I've done something
   wrong, God.
I want to tell you that
   I'm sorry.
Help me to say, "I'm sorry"
   to the person I hurt, too.
I want to do better next time.
Amen.

When I Go to Bed

Good night, God.
It's time for me to go to bed.
I know that you will take care of
   me while I'm sleeping.
This makes me feel so happy!
Please watch over my Mommy and
   Daddy and everyone I love.
Please watch over our world and
   all the people in it.
Thank you for this day, God.
I will talk to you again
   in the morning. Amen.

Printed in the United States
By Bookmasters